MW01245848

Steve, a former coal miner who spent years working at the coal face, raised a family of three with his wife Jane. Now, he enjoys writing about his life experiences, including humorous anecdotes from those formative years.

To my wife Jane and my sister Julie who encouraged me to write some poems. They both had more faith in me than I had in myself.

Stephen Howell

LIFE IS MOSTLY FUN

AUSTIN MACAULEY PUBLISHERS®

LONDON * CAMBRIDGE * NEW YORK * SHARJAH

Copyright © Stephen Howell 2024

The right of Stephen Howell to be identified as author of this work has been asserted by the author in accordance with sections 77 and 78 of the Copyright, Designs and Patents Act 1988.

All rights reserved. No part of this publication may be reproduced, stored in a retrieval system, or transmitted in any form or by any means, electronic, mechanical, photocopying, recording, or otherwise, without the prior permission of the publishers.

Any person who commits any unauthorised act in relation to this publication may be liable to criminal prosecution and civil claims for damages.

A CIP catalogue record for this title is available from the British Library.

ISBN 9781035873760 (Paperback)
ISBN 9781035873777 (ePub e-book)

www.austinmacauley.com

First Published 2024
Austin Macauley Publishers Ltd®
1 Canada Square
Canary Wharf
London
E14 5AA

Table of Contents

Our Land 9

Julie 10

Work 11

Camping 12

A Future 13

Winter 14

Driving These Days 15

Autumn 16

Sat Nav 17

Waiting 18

Spring 19

Mojo 20

Shopping 21

Alice Myths 22

Piano 23

Where Has Our Summers Gone 24

Pets 25

Kids Fun 26

Writing 27

Miss You 28

Plans 29

When Your Love Gives Me Life 30

Sight 31

One day 32

People 33

Smart 34

Packaging 35

Rocking 36

Yarns 37

Time 38

Art On Skin 39

The Receptionist 40

Our Land

This is the place where Dragons live
You may think that's not true
Cos on a cold dark winters night
I've seen more than just a few
They like to stay high in the sky
And barely out of sight
But if you look a little closer
You can see them all in flight
When a storm is raging
And the clouds are getting higher
It's not the lightning that you see
It's really Dragon fire
They live beneath the mountains
In the deepest darkest caves
So if you want to find them
You'd have to be so brave
But if you ever went down there
To that dark and scary place
You might just find some Dragons
And meet them face to face
But a Dragon wouldn't hurt you
On that you can depend
Because every Dragon always knows
Who wants to be a friend?
Some may like the highlands
Or might prefer the dales
But we live in the land of Dragons
And we all call it WALES

Julie

It's hard to find many words to say
Because I lost my sister yesterday
Her three daughters they have lost their mam
And are broken hearted every one
Your grandchildren that you loved so much
Will now grow up without nanny's touch
She was loud and mad and full of fun
And gave good advice to everyone
She didn't think about her self
But was happier helping everyone else
She loved her family and her pets
And to all of us you were one of the best
We all thought you would always be there
But now all we have is an empty chair
It's only now we realise
How much you filled up our lives
The hardest word it seems is goodbye
But you'll be with us for the rest of our lives
I don't think you could ever know how much you will be missed
So all of us will say to you night night and kiss kiss kiss!

Work

I started work upon my knees
Digging up Jurassic trees
Where every road was long and dark
And you wouldn't want to make a spark
They let me use a giant wheel
This wheel was made of teeth and steal
It ripped and tore through every shift
Jurassic trees could not resist
But when there spores choked up the air
We just worked on and didn't care
The pay that you were taking home
Just puts you in a comfort zone
Until the day you realise
That having riches is no prise
All the rewards that you receive
But they should have told you not to breath
Cos Jurassic spores like shards of glass
Could one day help to kill your asrse
So when your working days are through
You'll look back on the thing you do
But when I find it hard to breath
And sometimes if I cough and wheeze
It's digging up Jurassic trees
Has put me back down on my knees

Camping

We loved our holidays in the tent
It didn't matter where we went
By the sea or by a river
It didn't matter about the weather
We'd spend all day playing on the beach
With a picnic, ice cream and lots of treats
The kids wanted to try out a kite
But we couldn't get it to take flight
So I ran with it they thought that was fun
And all laughed like fools when I fell on my bum
But if it rained we didn't mind
We'd get in the car to see what we could find
Once we found a small reptile zoo
We had a guided tour that went right through
The kids just liked everything I think
And mam really loved the blue tongued skink
The guide took out a snake for us all to touch
Then we all heard mam say no thanks this is close enough
The evening times were really great
Playing cards and board games till quite late
One time we couldn't understand
Why the youngest of us won every hand
Then next day when we checked the pack
We found he'd bent the corners back
There really aren't any better days
Than with all the family on holidays

A Future

We once moved to a northern land
For a brighter future that we'd planned
It took some time to settle in
And wondered if we'd done the right thing
But when new friends start to come around
You can really start to settle down
The future looked bright like it did before
Until early March of 84
We all had a vote on that day
To stop them from taking our jobs away
Then it was time for me and those friends of mine
To take a stand on the picket line
Our wives were our rocks all through that time
Giving speeches and starting food lines
After that year our cause was lost
But when more years pass we count cost
Cos all the things we've lost since then
Will never come back ever again
The Rail, Steel, Shipyards and the Mines
Have been since then all in decline
Because all we wanted all through that strike
Was to keep everyone's future burning bright

Winter

The harshest of the seasons is winters icy grip
It turns puddles into glass so be careful you don't slip
Water that once dripped off the roof tip taping day and night
Has now been suddenly silenced and turned to transparent stalactites
Snowflakes look like butterflies fluttering all over the land
Even though you catch them you can't keep them in your hand
The summer birds have left looking for a place where warmth begins
They've flown away from winters touch for the sun upon their wings
When the snow has covered the bare trees it's such a pretty sight
It's just like that winter postcard that everybody likes
Kids can't wait for the snow to try out their new sleighs
They don't seem to feel the cold they'll be doing it for days
And when the winter snow comes it puts a smile on every face
Because everything looks cleaner roofs and roads and garden gates
Then we come to Christmas and kids want that special thing
But they'll just have to wait and see what Santa brings
They all hang up their stockings and hope they're filled up the top
And when they wake there's toys and sweets
There's really such a lot
Midwinter's celebration is to bring the New Year in
And all around the country people party dance and sing
The last thing we have in the winter months is our Valentine's
Day When everyone tries to show their love in a million different ways

Driving These Days

We go for a drive out in the car
It doesn't matter really how far
When you see some of the other drivers on the road
You could have a frustration overload
Some drive to close and keep dashing in and out
And haven't a clue when they come to a roundabout
There may be lane markings for everyone to share
But they'll just cut you up because they just don't really care
Some they drive too fast and some they're just to slow
You're sure to come across them wherever you may go
Some never indicate were they are going
Because they don't want anyone knowing
My daughter passed her test and got herself a car
I went out for a ride with her it wasn't very far
We came up to a roundabout I said pick a lane if you like
She replied now I've passed my test I can drive just where ever I like
Whether they can drive or not it really doesn't matter
It seems to me the way their driving to day they got their license from Christmas
cracker

Autumn

To soon the autumn days arrive and take over without warning
The light it fades and darkness takes over every morning
Leaves lose their green and put on Red and Brown now that it's started
They all fall down and cover the ground it is nature's autumn carpet
When all the leaves have gone and the trees are left so bare
Then autumn's cool touch comes and takes over in the air
Now it's time to put away all the summer things
So we'll dress a little warmer to see what the autumn brings
A warmer breakfast now it's time for some nice hot porridge
It's just the thing for cooler mornings when they're off to the collage of knowledge
Then soon all the crops are ready for the farmers harvest
And all the schools get ready for their festival of harvest
Now all the kids love to dress up for their spooky day
They go to scare the neighbours trick or treating all the way
Lots of families go to watch a firework's display
They try to keep tradition celebrating Guy forks Day
The 11th of the 11th is autumn's Remembrance Day
When a million poppy's always pave the way
In faraway fields poppy's flutter just like cotton
They bow their heads for all the ones that will never be forgotten

Sat Nav

We thought we'd try the satnav to go to a new destination
But when we finally got there it was the wrong location
Friends say to use the satnav because you can get there so much quicker
But when I tried to follow mine I nearly ended up in a river
I think it gets its messages from somewhere out in space
But what thing out in space could know the roads around this place
It doesn't know the new roads that are being built everywhere
It might be easier to ask a passer-by and they could direct you there
So you're driving down the road and the voice says left then says right
I hope we hurry up and get there it's the middle of the night
And coming up to roundabouts its exit one then it's three
I've had enough of roundabouts I'm starting to get dizzy
And any voice that you pick for your satnav doesn't sound too friendly
The voice it barks out orders like a Sargent in the army
So after all is said and done it might be better to catch a bus
Because buses go from A to B and there's hardly any fuss

Waiting

Why are we always waiting sometimes it's all we ever do
We waiting for the good things and perhaps some bad things to
You hang around all day that doesn't make it any better
Then the postman goes past the house and didn't bring the letter
When you're young you wait for the best of everything
Like Birthdays Summer Christmas and all the good things they can bring
But when you're a little older waiting's becomes something you can't stand
It's like someone's given you hour glass and filled it with slow sand
When you place an order and it says between days three and five
But after all the waiting you're order just don't arrive
You try to find your order but it's gone to outer space
I think they tell you three to five to put you in that waiting place
People say that they are coming and you have a time and day
Then they let you down but no apology comes your way
There's nothing worse than being let down at the final minute
It's like opening up a treasure chest and finding nothing in it
Some might say that waiting is a part of life i don't know if that's true
But sometimes the waiting just gets longer and there's nothing you can do
So if things just came on time and people turned up when they say
Then that could be the answer to make the waiting go away

Spring

We can't wait to welcome the first days of spring
And all the wonder's that it brings
The sun it comes up earlier and the days are little longer
And more of that special spring sunshine makes everything much stronger
Young buds and flowers raise their heads
Awakened from their sleepy beds
They twist and push until they break free
It's such an amazing sight to see
Soon every were has a dash of colour
As they all break free of winters' umbrella
And know nest building on every bird's mind
With twigs and straw and bits of twine
They finish their nests in time it took so much
But know it's ready for a brand new clutch
The hatchlings have an enormous appetite
It keeps mam and dad in constant flight
We check the fields when we're driving around
To see if any new lambs can be found
Then we finally spot quite a few
It's another part of spring that's young and new
While children sleep Easter Bunny comes around
And leaves Easter Eggs for all the children in the town
Then we'll all embark on an Easter egg trail
Be sure to check all the buckets and every pail
It's a magical season when it begins
These are some of the reasons we all love spring

Mojo

I think I lost my mojo I just don't know where it may be
It could be in the garden perhaps hiding in a tree
I don't know why my mojo would want to hide away from me
You can't taste or touch it and it's very hard to see
I know I had it Monday but on Tuesday it was gone
I really hope my mojo doesn't stay away to long
I've got to search and find it because without it I'm no good
And I have the strangest feeling that my heart is made of wood
So I'll check around the house again and hope it reappears
I know that i can't see it but I'll feel it when it's near
Your mojo is the strangest thing where it comes from now one knows
But your lost and fall to pieces every time it goes
So when my mojo comes back I'll hold on to it real tight
And hope there isn't another time that my mojo just takes flight
So if you're mojo leaves you will hope it's only for a while
Because when you have your mojo it's the thing that helps you smile

Shopping

I do my shopping at the local superstore
They seem to be building more and more
They're building a new one down the road on the right
And when this one's open you can shop all night
I always get the trolley with the wonky wheel
And I bet you can guess how that would feel
It rattles and squeaks all around the shop
Even a gallon of oil couldn't make it stop
They really should provide a crèche
Because kids leave the shop in a terrible mess
They like to press the buttons on all the new toys
Because some are not happy unless they're making a noise
People stop and block the middle of the aisle
They chat with friends they haven't seen for a while
You can try and get past them but there's just no way
It's easier to turn around and go back the other way
I once met a giant in aisle 33
He must been a giant he was four feet taller than me
I said to him are you a giant man
He looked down from above and said, 'YES I AM'

Alice Myths

If Alice went through the looking glass
Then why won't mine just let me pass
To go on through that guarded gate
Where myth and magic may lie in wait
So should I dream and fantasise
Of all the things that hide inside
Will I have to get into a strange habit?
Of playing hide and seek with a big white rabbit
Would Hare and Hater share their tea?
I suppose I'll have to wait and see
Will a Cats grin help me on my way?
Or would it be better to find myself another way!
If I met the Tweeddale twins that would be a surprise
And would the stories that they tell just be contrary-wise
To see that creature with lots of legs with his question who are you
It must be hard with all those legs to tie up all those shoes
Then perhaps I'll hear that voice that screams out off with their heads
And that's when I feel so lucky that I wake up in my bed
Because fantasies are timeless and so are all our dreams
But perhaps one day we'll find out what they really mean

Piano

I'd like to lay my hands upon the keys
And play some chords and melodies
I wonder how good it could be
To play a song in any key
I tried some books to help me out
But only confusion fell about
I search for tutors on the internet
But I haven't found a good one yet
They like to show how clever they are
But that won't help me get very far
It makes me think old dog new tricks
But I'll keep on trying till something clicks
So I learn a few chords and master them quick
And now all I need is a song that fits
Perhaps I'll write and play my own song
Then no one would know if I'm playing it wrong
Music may be a language that's really hard to understand
But one day when I work it out I could be a piano man

Where Has Our Summers Gone

The September moon sits in the sky
To another summer we say goodbye
It's not the same as when we were young
It seemed every day was filled with sun
We couldn't wait for May to come
When the outdoor pools opened up for fun
There was sun and picnics by the pool
It's a pity we had to go back to school
I must admit we had some afternoons off school
So we could spend more time down at the pool
And when the school term finely ends
And we were set free with all our friends
Then we knew that summer had arrived
With the brilliant sunshine from the sky
To be in the park with all your friends
Having great fun and making dens
We had a piece of cardboard to slide down the mountain
And had our drinks from a freshwater fountain
There was an old rope swing across the river
The first drop from the swing the water made us shiver
We'd sneak some fruit from garden patches
And then we'd run and hide so they didn't catch us
We went on bus trips down to the sea
And we couldn't wait to spend our 50p
Summers back then were so much fun
We were young and there was so much sun

Pets

We thought we'd get some little pets and breed them just for fun
But what we didn't realise is that we could get overrun
So we looked around the pet shops and went to quite a few
And we found these brown fluffy rodents and they were called Degu's
The man in the pet shop said that Degu's are just right
He said they're very friendly and hardly ever bite
So we got some boys and girls and soon the breeding had began
And it wasn't very long before the place was overrun
We built a few more cages for all the new arrivals
And started to supply the pet shops or we'd have been up to our eyeballs
We couldn't keep the young ones in they were running round the house
And any visitor that we had said do you know I'm sure I seen a mouse
Then we had some trouble with all the power tripping out
We needed to call an electrician of that there was no doubt
So when the electrician came and that cost a bit of money
He said that there was nothing wrong and that bit wasn't funny
Then after a few more months went by with the power off and on
It was obvious to us that there was clearly something wrong
Then I was walking past the fridge one day I heard a funny noise
So I pulled it out to look at the back and there to my surprise
Every wire in the fridge had been stripped down to its core
And you'd think with all that damage it wouldn't be working anymore
But even with that bit of trouble Degu's breeding was great fun
They were furry funny and friendly and we'd recommend them to anyone

Kids Fun

I remember when our kids were young and everything was new and fun
Like teaching them to walk and talk and teaching then to run
I taught them how to catch a ball it's really not that hard
At least you wouldn't think it was until three hours in the yard
And then we tried a bat and ball well that was even worse
The bat just had a mind of its own and
I'm sure the ball was cursed
We tried a bigger bat and a bigger ball
But even that didn't help at all
It didn't matter how many times you missed
You just kept saying I can do this
Then one day it all fell in to place
And you were hitting the ball all over the place
You said I can hit it now Dad look how far
As the ball bounced off the neighbours car
We laugh about it to this day
How the ball kept getting away
The time we spent I would never replace
Just to see the pleasure on your face

Writing

I guess sometimes you come to a wall
And you don't know what to write at all
If you try to hard it's too much pressure
And that doesn't make it any better
Then you think you have an idea
But the book and pen is nowhere near
It bounces around your head all day
And then suddenly it goes away
You won't to have the idea back
But it's in your head somewhere at the back
It's hard to find what you wanted to say
With all the other stuff in the way
So you lay in bed it's dark and quiet
Then all the words they start a riot
And when the noise starts to fade away
It's time to focus on another day
Today is going to be much better
With ideas hanging on every letter
And when the words just start to flow
It makes me wonder where they go
But now their back I'm feeling alright
I think I'll write all day and night
So the next time I come to that wall
I don't think I will stress at all
I'll just wait until the words come back
And then my writing is back on track

Miss You

I'm a broken hearted weekend dad
When Monday to Friday feels so bad
I hardly ever see your face
Cos I wake up in a different place
Two days just aren't long enough
To try and do the normal stuff
Like brush your hair or tie your shoe
There should be something I can do
So we'll go for fast food and a toy
That brings us both a little joy
I shop all week for some nice things
So I can see the smile it brings
I'll have your laughter and your smiles
It makes me feel like daddy for a while
I'm spending too much time alone
I really wish I could come back home
Because there's nothing that is quite as sad
As a broken hearted weekend dad

Plans

I always say we shouldn't make plans
Because life jumps in with meddling hands
A simple plan has steps one and two
Then trouble just comes crashing through
If the plan is big or if it's small
Mayhem steps in to shatter it all
You think your plan might run smooth this time
But chaos is coming close behind
And even if your plan feels right
Bad luck comes to take a bite
So if forward planning is your thing
I'll only add just one more thing
If any plan goes right one day
I probably wouldn't know what to say

When Your Love Gives Me Life

Ever since I touched your skin
There's been a fire that burns within
The light you gave me burns so bright
It's enough to last me all my life
Fate is the one that put us together
So we both know it'll last forever
When we were young we made a pact

To always have each other's backs
Then time moves on now we know it's true
That you love me and I love you
If i was the man I wished I could be
I'd open your eyes and help you see
That fire and light burn bright together
And the love we have will last forever

Thank you x

Sight

I wonder if we've ever been told
How the universe unfolds
There's so many things that we don't know
About a place we'll never go
We should move our sights back to the ground
And then we might see what could be found
But it seems that some can never see
How easy things could really be
If black and white is always right
Then why is it we have to fight
From day to day and year to year
It feels as if we live in fear
What can we do to stop the dread?
Perhaps use our hearts and not our heads
All the things that life can bring
But do we really learn a thing
It seems to me that hearts and minds
Have always been on opposite sides
But if one day they came together
There won't be as much stormy weather

One day

I always wished I could write a song
Like all the hits by Paul and John
Cos every song they wrote together
We all know will last forever
Like Elton J and Bernie T
Yes
they're songs just inspire me
When every song comes from the heart
Please someone help me make a start
The verses and chorus there could be
Perhaps it's just eluding me
To put some meaningful words together
Maybe I'm just not that clever
If I could find the building block
That one day makes the whole world rock
But is that aiming far too high
Because I'm just a normal guy
I'll write some words I think might rhyme
And hope some music falls in line
You never know it might click one day
And then a song could come my way

People

We sometimes like to people watch it's something that we do
So if you want to have a laugh just sit and do it to
I've noticed something about these days
That people have such funny ways
Wearing shorts all through the winter that just can't be right
And if I ever did that I'd end up with frost bite
We've seen dogs in pushchairs yest it's true
Just look around you'll see it to
Heard rebellious children screaming all around the shop
The mam just looks oblivious cos she can't make it stop
Mischievous dogs that tie their owners up in nots
And young families with lots of unruly little tots
So when your out and about and have a look around
Then you might just see some of what I've written down
There's one thing to remember if your people watching to
There might be someone out there having a laugh at YOU

Smart

Everything is smart these days
At least that's what the clever ones say
Your phone can hold a million apps
If you've got a spare year you can browse them perhaps
You have a watch that can Internet stream
When all you need is the time on the screen
Most of us have a smart tv
I have one and it's smarter than me
There are cars that run on electricity
But how do you change the batteries
People go to work using laptops in their houses
They work in their pyjamas no need to put on trousers
There's loads of technology for boys and girls
Who can play their games in virtual worlds
Perhaps my high tec is from way back when
Because I'm alright with a pad and a pen

Packaging

I think I'll write a little note
Perhaps we'll end it with a joke
All the packaging there is today
And so much that we throw away
Some of the packets so tightly sealed
We need to give a sword a wield
Milk bottle tabs that just brake off
You'll need knife to get the top off
Crisp packets that are full of air
Burst them open crisps everywhere
Boxes covered in sticky tape
Try and pull it but it just won't break
The worst one out of all of these
Is trying to open a block of cheese
There's an easy open tear off top
All I'll say to that there really is not
You turn the packet round and round
But the opening just cannot be found
The best thing you can do with these
Is pass it to someone else and say
OPEN THIS UP PLEASE!

Rocking

We listen to some tracks as loud as they will play
We can't wait to play them it's another rocking day
We love to hear the sounds from the time when we were younger
As long as it is loud and the speakers shake with thunder
You need to have the bass and treble really blasting out
Cos when you tune it up it's louder than the devil's shout
And when the lead guitar rips through another riff
That is when you realise it can't get better than this
So you can tell that we are rockers I'm very glad to say
And we're gonna keep on rocking every single day

Yarns

I wonder if you've heard a story
All about blood and all about glory
For that would be the worst kind of story
Because where there's blood there is no glory
If a sacred path is the one you take
How will you know if you've made a mistake
Because the path of life is the one we all take
And we should all learn from our mistakes
We've all heard tales of brave and bold
And how things can be bought and sold
To live your life is brave and bold
Cos experience can't be bought or sold
There are ancient yarns of mystery and magic
Do you crave these things just like an addict
Because life's a mystery and love is magic
So let's all treasure these things like an addict

Time

I sometimes get so lost at night
Should I pick up the guitar or shall I write
Will I play a game with friends online
Or would that be just a waste of time
Perhaps I'll turn the tv on
And watch the repeats go on and on
I might watch a movie from the past
Don't know how long my interest will last
Shall I listen to music through headphones
Perhaps that's an idea so nobody moans
So I'll watch the cars go down the road
And then I'll know I'm already bored
So if another night starts like this
I think I'll give the boredom a miss
Cos now it's time to focus my mind
Instead of wasting so much time

Art On Skin

Why do people look down on art on skin
Cos I think it's a beautiful thing
Why not enhance your looks
With pictures and words from fantasy books
Have the lyrics from your favourite song
It'll be there to last your whole life long
Whether it's flowers or a pirate ship
Or something delicate on your hip
There could be something you've always wanted done
Like the name of your daughter or the name of your son
Some people like to show how patriotic they can be
By having a flag of their beloved country
From unicorns to skulls with horns
It makes no difference the choice is yours
Because art on skin is here to stay
So make your choice on a tattoo today

The Receptionist

I went to try and see the Doctor the other day
But according to the receptionist this is really not the way
You have to go home and phone me and we'll see what we can do
We might get the Doc to phone you back but in a day or two
So I go back home to phone them and it's option 1 or 2
But you can't talk to a human because your 20 minutes in a queue
Then she asked me all my symptoms but she's just a receptionist
And then she says it might be quicker to speak to the pharmacist
So I stick to my guns because it's the Doc I want to see
But to get face to face with Doc could take a week or three
So if you're feeling ill or your tummy's in a twist
You could get in to see the Doc if you get past the receptionist

Printed in the USA
CPSIA information can be obtained
at www.ICGtesting.com
CBHW040236231024
16239CB00062B/1020